Fun Fan Facts:
The Unofficial NBA Edition

Portland Trail Blazers

Everything Young Trail Blazers
Fans Should Know

By: Jake Liam

Dedication

To every Trail Blazers fan who has ever screamed "RIP CITY!" at the top of their lungs and did not care one bit who was watching.

And to Damian Lillard, who proved that buzzer-beaters hit different when the whole city is holding its breath. Dame Time was never just a catchphrase. It was a feeling.

This one is for Rip City. Keep blazing.

THE NBA BY THE NUMBERS

MOST NBA CHAMPIONSHIPS*

CELTICS (18) †

LAKERS (17)

WARRIORS (7)

BULLS (6)

SPURS (5)

As of the 2024-25 Season. † One Trophy = 4 Championships.

BIG NUMBERS

$156 million
Stephen Curry's est. earnings in the 24-25 season

7'7"
Tallest player in NBA history (Gheorghe Mureşan & Manute Bol)

NBA HISTORY SNAPSHOT

1946 NBA Founded

1954 Shot Clock Introduced

1979 3-Point Line Added

2023 NBA Cup Introduced

30 | 4 | 82

Teams Competing in the NBA

Playoff Rounds

Games Per Season

EASTERN CONFERENCE

Atlantic – **Celtics**
Atlantic – **Nets**
Atlantic – **Knicks**
Atlantic – **76ers**
Atlantic – **Raptors**
Central – **Bulls**
Central – **Cavaliers**
Central – **Pistons**
Central – **Pacers**
Central – **Bucks**
Southeast – **Hawks**
Southeast – **Hornets**
Southeast – **Heat**
Southeast – **Magic**
Southeast – **Wizards**

WESTERN CONFERENCE

Pacific – **Lakers**
Pacific – **Clippers**
Pacific – **Warriors**
Pacific – **Suns**
Pacific – **Kings**
Northwest – **Nuggets**
Northwest – **Timberwolves**
Northwest – **Thunder**
Northwest – **Trail Blazers**
Northwest – **Jazz**
Southwest – **Mavericks**
Southwest – **Rockets**
Southwest – **Spurs**
Southwest – **Pelicans**
Southwest – **Grizzlies**

PORTLAND TRAILBLAZERS
IN THE NBA

- FOUNDED: 1970 †
- NBA TITLES: 1
- CONFERENCE TITLES: 3*

36 Playoff Appearances

*† Founding dates are complicated & may cause arguments at Thanksgiving. Ask someone born before color TV. All Titles reflect pre-relocation franchise history. * As of 2024-25 Season.*

NBA ALL-TIME MVP LEADERS

KAREEM ABDUL-JABBAR (6) ★ MICHAEL JORDAN (5) ★ BILL RUSSELL (5)

Introduction

Welcome, fans! Whether you're new to cheering for the Portland Trail Blazers or you've been bleeding the team colors your whole life, this book is packed with fun, exciting facts about your favorite team. Get ready to impress your friends and family with everything you know about the Trail Blazers.

Quick Timeout

This book is packed with stats. Like, A LOT of stats. Every fact was checked, double-checked, and triple-checked. But here's the thing about basketball history: not everyone agrees on everything. Ask someone who watched games before color TV and someone who grew up with instant replay and you'll get two completely different answers. My dad, stepdad, uncle, and grandpa all argued about the same fact. Four people. Four answers. All of them think they're right. So if you spot something that doesn't match what you've heard, congratulations. You might be a bigger fan than the people who helped make this book. And honestly? That's pretty cool.

HOW IT WORKS

THE SEASON
82 Games. One Goal.
Each team plays 82 games.
Win enough to make the
Playoffs.
Every game counts!

PLAYOFFS
30 Teams. 16 Make It.
8 per conference make the playoffs.
Win=Advance | Lose=Go Home
Best record
gets home court!

PLAYOFF ROUNDS
Best of 7. Win 4 or Go Home.
4 rounds of pure pressure.
Every series is do-or-die!

OVERTIME?
5 More Minutes.
Keep playing until
someone pulls ahead.
No ties. Ever.

THE FINALS
One Series. One Champion.
Winner lifts the Trophy.
Legend status unlocked.

How the NBA Works

At first glance, basketball feels simple. Ten players. One ball. Two hoops. Go.

Then the NBA adds the layers.

An 82-game regular season. A draft where bad teams pick first. Playoffs that last two full months. Superstars who can change everything with one trade. Dynasties that rise, fall, and rise again.

And somehow, it all works.

The NBA is built on one big idea: every team gets a chance to reset, reload, and rise again. No relegation. No dropping down to a lower league. Just basketball, every night, from October through June.

It is a league designed for drama, stars, and comebacks. And once you understand the flow, it is impossible to stop watching.

The League Setup

The NBA has 30 teams, spread across the United States and Canada. Those teams are split into two conferences:

- Eastern Conference
- Western Conference

Each conference has three divisions, mostly based on geography. Divisions matter for scheduling, but not as much as they used to.

Every team plays 82 regular season games, usually from October through April. Home games. Road games. Back-to-back nights. Long road trips. The season is a marathon before the sprint even starts.

Win games, and you climb the standings. Lose too many, and the pressure builds fast.

How Games Are Played

An NBA game has four quarters, each lasting 12 minutes. That means 48 minutes of game time, plus timeouts, free throws, and the occasional coach argument that adds another 20 minutes nobody planned for.

Scoring is simple:

- A shot inside the three-point line is worth 2 points
- A shot beyond the arc is worth 3 points
- Free throws are worth 1 point

If the score is tied at the end of regulation, the game goes to overtime, which lasts 5 minutes. Still tied? Another overtime. Keep going until someone wins.

There is a shot clock too. Teams have 24 seconds to take a shot. No standing around. No holding the ball forever. Keep it moving.

The Regular Season Race

The regular season is long for a reason. It tests everything.

Depth. Health. Focus. Patience.

Teams play opponents from both conferences, but they face conference rivals more often. By the end of the season, each conference's top teams have earned their playoff spots the hard way.

The goal is simple: make the playoffs. But there is a twist.

The NBA Cup

In 2023, the NBA added something new to the middle of the season. Something with actual stakes. They called it the In-Season Tournament, now known as the NBA Cup.

It works like this: Every team plays a small group stage during November and December, with special court designs that look like nothing else in basketball. The best teams advance to a knockout round held in Las Vegas.

The winners split a prize pool. Players earn bonus money. And for the first time, a team could lift a trophy before the playoffs even started.

Some fans are still warming up to it. Some players love it. But the moment a team starts treating it seriously and a crowd shows up buzzing in December, it feels like something.

Which, honestly, sounds about right.

The Play-In Tournament

Instead of sending the top eight teams from each conference straight to the playoffs, the NBA added something new. The Play-In Tournament.

Here is how it works:

- Teams ranked 1 through 6 in each conference are safe
- Teams ranked 7 through 10 fight for the final two playoff spots

The 7 and 8 seeds have an advantage. Win once and you are in. Lose and you still get one more shot. The 9 and 10 seeds have to win twice in a row just to earn a first-round matchup.

It turns the end of the season into a sprint. Every game suddenly matters more. Fans love it. Coaches age rapidly.

The NBA Playoffs

Once the playoffs begin, everything tightens.

Sixteen teams enter. Eight from each conference. Every round is a best-of-seven games series. That means the first team to win four games moves on:

- First Round
- Conference Semifinals
- Conference Finals
- NBA Finals

Home-court advantage matters. Crowds get louder. Rotations get shorter. Superstars play heavier minutes. One bad quarter can flip a series. One great performance can define a career.

By the time the NBA Finals arrive in June, only two teams are left. One from the East. One from the West. Four wins away from a championship. Four wins away from history.

The NBA Draft: Hope Begins Here

Here is where the NBA gets clever. Every summer, new players enter the league through the NBA Draft. Teams take turns selecting college players, international stars, and teenagers straight out of high school.

The teams that finished with the worst records get the best odds to pick early through the Draft Lottery. It is not guaranteed, but it gives struggling franchises a real shot at changing their future with one pick.

That means one bad season does not doom you forever. It might actually change everything. Some franchises are rebuilt by a single draft night moment.

Hope shows up wearing a new jersey.

No Relegation. All Pressure.

Unlike many global sports leagues, NBA teams never drop down to a lower league. They always stay in the NBA.

That does not mean there is no pressure.

Fans remember losing seasons. Owners make changes. Coaches get replaced. Players get traded. Every year is a test of direction, patience, and belief.

Stars, Systems, and Showtime

The NBA is famous for its stars. But stars do not win alone.

Teams need chemistry. Coaches need systems. Role players need to deliver on the biggest stages. One injury. One hot streak. One trade deadline deal. Any of it can flip a season.

That balance between individual brilliance and team basketball is what makes the league special.

Fast breaks. Buzzer-beaters. Game 7s. And moments that get replayed forever. That is the NBA.

Once you get the flow, it is pure electricity.

Portland Trail Blazers Facts

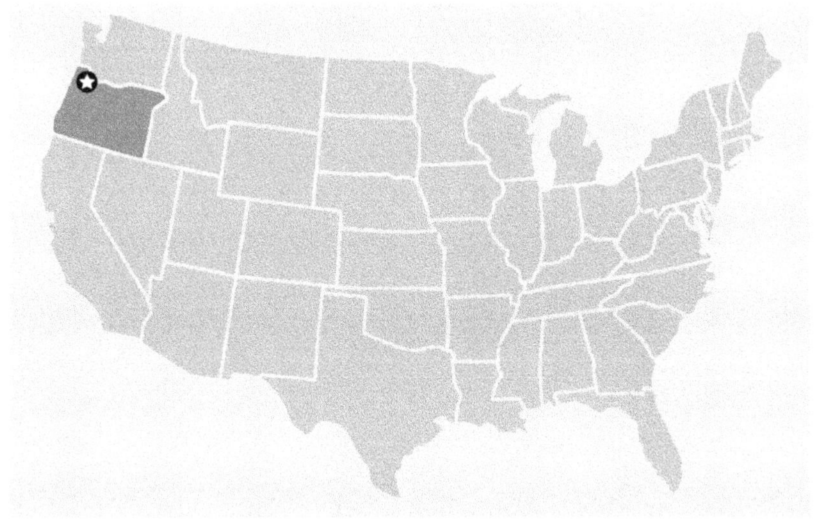

Home City

Portland, Oregon

Metro Area Population

About 2.5 Million

Home Arena

Moda Center

Arena Capacity

19,393

Conference / Division

Western Conference / Northwest Division

Famous Local Food

Voodoo Doughnut, Dungeness crab, hazelnuts,
Tillamook cheese

Chapter 1: Rip City Rising

1. Born in Oregon

In 1970, the NBA decided to expand, and Portland, Oregon raised its hand so fast it practically dislocated a shoulder. The city had been angling for a pro sports team for years, and when the league announced it was adding new franchises, Portland came through with the entry fee, the arena plans, and enough enthusiasm to power a small city. Which, conveniently, is exactly what Portland was.

The Trail Blazers played their very first game on October 16, 1970, beating the Cleveland Cavaliers 115-112. Two expansion teams. One game. Zero defense from either side. Jim Barnett led Portland with 31 points, rookie Geoff Petrie chipped in 21, and the Blazers came from behind in the fourth quarter to win it at Memorial Coliseum in front of 4,273 fans who had absolutely no idea they were witnessing history. It was, by most accounts, not a basketball clinic. But Portland was officially in the NBA, and they had started it with a win. Oregonians had waited long enough, and the basketball gods at least had the decency to reward their patience on night one.

What made Portland's entry into the league interesting was the name itself. "Trail Blazers" was chosen through a public contest, a nod to the pioneers and explorers who had traveled the Oregon Trail westward in the 1800s. Other finalists included the Pioneers, the Aces, and the Explorers. Portland went with Trail Blazers. The right call. Imagine cheering for the Portland Aces. Actually, do not.

2. Where Did "Rip City" Come From?

This is one of the greatest accidental traditions in all of professional sports, and it happened because a broadcaster got excited and said something that made absolutely no logical sense.

It was 1971. The Blazers were playing at home. Guard Jim Barnett launched a long shot that splashed through the net, and radio announcer Bill Schonely, caught completely off guard by the beauty of it, blurted out "Rip City!" into his microphone. He had never said it before. He did not have a plan for what it meant. He just said it, it sounded electric, and it stuck to Portland like rain in November. Which, in Portland, is saying something.

Schonely himself has said over the years that he still is not entirely sure where it came from. Some people have tried to attach meaning to it after the fact. None of the explanations are particularly convincing. And honestly, that makes it better. "Rip City" does not need a definition. It is a feeling. It is the sound of a sold-out arena losing its mind when the home team does something unforgettable. It is Portland's version of a battle cry, born in one spontaneous, beautiful, slightly confused moment in 1971 and still going strong today.

3. Building a Winner

The early Trail Blazers were, to put it kindly, a work in progress. To put it less kindly, they lost a lot of games in ways that were impressive in their consistency. Their first few seasons featured a rotating cast of players who were trying hard, fans who were trying harder, and a front office that was learning on the job right along with everyone else.

But in 1976, Portland hired a coach named Jack Ramsay, a man who looked like your favorite history teacher but coached basketball like someone had personally offended him. Ramsay was a tactician, a disciplinarian, and exactly the kind of steady hand the franchise needed. He started building something. It was slow. It was not glamorous. It involved a lot of film sessions and a lot of defensive drills. But piece by piece, the roster started to take shape.

The turning point came in the 1974 NBA Draft, when Portland selected guard Lionel Hollins, followed by more savvy moves that brought together a group of players who genuinely liked each other and genuinely wanted to win. Nobody outside of Oregon was paying much attention yet. That was fine. Portland was busy building something nobody saw coming.

4. The 1977 Championship

Imagine this: it is Game 6 of the 1977 NBA Finals. The Portland Trail Blazers, a franchise that had never won anything, that was only seven years old, that played in a city most basketball fans could not find on a map, are four quarters away from a championship. The Philadelphia 76ers, led by Julius "Dr. J" Erving, are standing in the way. The Moda Center predecessor, Memorial Coliseum, is so loud the building is practically vibrating.

Portland won. They absolutely won. The Trail Blazers defeated the 76ers four games to two, and the city of

Portland erupted in a celebration that people who were there still talk about like it happened last week. Bill Walton, the big red-headed center who had completely dominated the series, was named Finals MVP. Jack Ramsay, the history-teacher coach who had believed in this group the whole time, pumped his fist so hard it probably hurt for a week.

Here is the part that makes Blazers fans both proud and a little bit sad: that championship in 1977 is still the only one Portland has ever won. One title. One banner. One perfect season that the entire city has been chasing ever since. But here is the thing about having one championship, one legendary run, one perfect moment frozen in time. You never stop talking about it. And Portland never has.

5. Bill Walton: The Big Red Machine

Bill Walton was six feet eleven inches tall, had hair like a rock musician, and played basketball with the kind of joy that made opponents genuinely frustrated because you cannot really be mad at someone who looks like they are having the time of their life while beating you. Walton was the centerpiece of that 1977 championship team, and calling him "good" would be like calling the Pacific Ocean "damp."

Walton was named the NBA's Most Valuable Player for the 1977-78 season, and during that championship run he was arguably the best player in the entire league. His passing was extraordinary for a center, his defense was suffocating, and he had a basketball IQ that coaches dream about. He understood the game at a level that most players take a decade to reach. Walton reached it in his mid-twenties, in Portland, in front of fans who treated him like he had personally delivered the championship by hand.

The sad part of the Walton story, and it is genuinely sad, is that injuries derailed what should have been an all-time great career. Foot problems kept him off the court for long stretches, and Portland never quite recaptured that championship magic after he left. But for one glorious stretch in the mid-to-late 1970s, Bill Walton was exactly what Rip City needed. A giant, red-haired, basketball genius who loved Portland right back. The city has never forgotten him, and it never will.

Bill Walton throws his arms wide in pure emotion. Long hair flying. Voice raised to the arena. In the late 1970s Walton powered the Portland Trail Blazers to their first NBA championship in 1977 and became one of basketball's most unforgettable big men. *Photo: Bill Walton with the Portland Trail Blazers. Photograph via Wikimedia Commons. Licensed under CC BY-SA 2.0. Source: Wikimedia Commons.*

6. Clyde Drexler: The Glide (1983-1995)

There are players who are smooth, and then there was Clyde Drexler, a man who appeared to move through basketball games the way a hot knife moves through butter. Effortlessly. Quietly. And leaving a very clean path of destruction behind him. Drexler earned the nickname "The Glide" because his movement on the court was so fluid it looked like he was operating under different rules of gravity than everyone else. Spoiler: he basically was.

Drexler spent eleven seasons in Portland, from 1983 to 1995, and during that time he became the face of the franchise in a way that very few players ever become the face of anything. He was a six-time All-Star as a Blazer, a relentless scorer, a lockdown defender when he wanted to be, and a player so gifted that the 1992 Olympic Dream Team, which contained a roster of humans widely considered to be the greatest basketball collection ever assembled, looked at Clyde Drexler and said yes, him, absolutely, he belongs here. He did.

The one thing Portland fans still think about when they think about Clyde is the 1992 Finals, which we will get to in Chapter 3 and which still stings a little. But Drexler's legacy in Portland is not defined by what did not happen. It is defined by eleven years of breathtaking basketball, a number 22 jersey hanging in the rafters, and a nickname so perfect it sounds like it was invented by a marketing team but was actually just the honest truth. The man glided. It was not a metaphor.

7. Terry Porter: T-Port (1985-1995)

If Clyde Drexler was the face of those late-eighties and early-nineties Blazer teams, Terry Porter was the brain. And the engine. And the guy who quietly made everything work while Drexler got the highlight packages and the magazine covers. Porter was the kind of player that coaches love, teammates trust, and casual fans consistently underrate, which is one of the great injustices in Trail Blazers history.

Porter played ten seasons in Portland and was the starting point guard on both of the Blazers' Finals teams, in 1990 and 1992. He averaged over seventeen points per game during his peak years, shot the three-pointer at a level that was considered elite for his era, and ran the offense with the calm confidence of someone who had definitely already seen every defense you were going to throw at him. Terry Porter was not flashy. He was better than flashy. He was reliable, and in basketball, reliable wins games.

Here is a fun way to understand Terry Porter's importance. Imagine a restaurant where Clyde Drexler is the spectacular main course that everyone orders and talks about. Terry Porter is the kitchen. Without him, nothing gets to the table. The Blazers of that era were genuinely one of the best teams in the NBA, a Western Conference powerhouse that went toe to toe with the Chicago Bulls for a championship and came agonizingly close. Porter was at the controls both times. He deserves considerably more credit than he typically receives, and if you are ever in a conversation with a Blazers fan of a certain age, just say "Terry Porter was underrated" and watch their eyes light up like you have said something sacred.

8. Arvydas Sabonis: Sabo (1995-2003)

Here is a fact that will genuinely bother you once you understand it. Arvydas Sabonis, the Lithuanian center who played for Portland from 1995 to 2003, was widely considered one of the most skilled big men in the history of basketball. Seven feet tall. Could pass like a point guard. Could shoot from the perimeter. Had footwork that made opposing centers look like they were learning to walk for the first time. Basketball people who watched him in Europe in the 1980s still talk about him with the reverence usually reserved for people who have done something historically significant.

Portland drafted Sabonis in 1986. He did not arrive until 1995, nine years later, because of the Soviet sports system, injuries, and roughly a decade's worth of complicated international basketball politics. By the time he got to the NBA, he was thirty-one years old, had two surgically repaired Achilles tendons, and moved around the court at a pace that was generously described as "deliberate." And he was still one of the most dominant big men in the Western Conference.

Imagine what Sabonis would have been at twenty-two, fully healthy, in the NBA. Basketball historians have been having that argument for decades. Some people believe he would have been the greatest center of his generation. Others believe he would have been better than that. Nobody will ever know, which is both the tragedy and the legend of Arvydas Sabonis. He showed up to Portland with knees that had been through a war, gave the Blazers eight good years, and still managed to be remarkable. That is either the most impressive thing you have ever heard or the most frustrating. Possibly both at the same time.

9. LaMarcus Aldridge: LMA (2006-2015)

LaMarcus Aldridge did not do anything loudly. He did not trash talk. He did not celebrate extravagantly. He did not generate tabloid headlines or post controversial things or show up to press conferences wearing something that caused a national conversation. What LaMarcus Aldridge did, consistently, for nine seasons in Portland, was score basketball points in volumes that were almost unfair, and he did it so efficiently and so quietly that some people did not fully appreciate what they were watching until he was gone.

Aldridge was a six-time All-Star, five of those selections coming during his time with the Blazers. He was a mid-range scoring machine at a time when the mid-range jumper was being declared extinct, a living, breathing argument that footwork and fundamentals never actually go out of style. His back-to-the-basket game was a throwback to a different era of basketball, polished and precise and extremely difficult to stop even when opposing coaches drew up specific plans to stop it.

The thing about Aldridge that Portland fans know, even if the rest of the country was slow to catch on, is that he carried the franchise. For years, during rebuilding stretches and roster transitions, he was the reason people still showed up. He was not the flashiest reason. He was not the loudest reason. But he was a reliable, excellent, professional basketball player who gave Portland everything he had for nearly a decade, and when he left for San Antonio in 2015, the city felt it. Even quietly. Especially quietly.

10. Damian Lillard: Dame Dolla (2012-2023)

Dame Time is not a real thing on a clock. There is no official Dame Time hour. No watchmaker has produced a Dame Time edition. And yet, if you ask anyone who watched Damian Lillard play basketball for the Portland Trail Blazers between 2012 and 2023, they will tell you that Dame Time is absolutely real, it is terrifying if you are on the wrong team, and it tends to arrive at exactly the moment when you thought you had the game under control.

Lillard was drafted sixth overall in 2012 and immediately became one of those players who the league knew was special before the league wanted to admit it out loud. He was from Oakland. He went to Weber State, which is not exactly a school that produces NBA legends on a regular basis. He played in Portland, which the national sports media visits approximately once every three years. None of that stopped him. Lillard won Rookie of the Year in 2013, made six All-Star teams as a Blazer, and became arguably the greatest player in franchise history by doing things with a basketball in clutch moments that genuinely did not seem physically possible.

The buzzer-beater against Oklahoma City in 2019 is the headline, and we will cover that properly in Chapter 3 where it belongs. But the full Damian Lillard story in Portland is bigger than any single shot. It is about a player who chose a small market and made it feel like the center of the basketball universe every time he stepped on the floor. It is about loyalty and confidence and the very specific kind of courage it takes to take the big shot, in the big moment, with the whole city watching, and believe so completely that it is going in that you are already pointing at the crowd before it lands. Dame Time was never on the clock. It was in the man.

Chapter 3: Moments That Made Rip City Lose Its Mind

11. The 1992 Finals: So Close It Still Hurts

The Portland Trail Blazers of the early 1990s were legitimately one of the best teams in the NBA. Not "pretty good for a small market" best. Not "impressive considering" best. Actually, genuinely, keep-opposing-coaches-up-at-night best. They won sixty games in the 1991-92 regular season. Sixty. They had Drexler, Porter, power forward Kevin Duckworth, and a roster so deep and well-constructed that neutral basketball observers looked at them and quietly said "yeah, this might be the year Portland wins it all."

Then they ran into the Chicago Bulls. Specifically, they ran into Michael Jordan, Scottie Pippen, and Phil Jackson, which is roughly the basketball equivalent of preparing your whole life for a swimming race and showing up to find out your competitor is a dolphin. The Bulls were in the middle of their first three-peat, operating at a level of basketball excellence that was frankly inconsiderate to every other team in the league. Game 1 of the Finals featured Jordan hitting six three-pointers in the first half alone, after which he turned to the courtside camera and shrugged in a way that communicated both "I do not know what is happening either" and "yes I absolutely do."

Portland pushed the series to six games and had real moments where a different outcome felt possible. They won Games 3 and 4 in Portland, and Rip City was absolutely electric. Then the Bulls closed it out in Game 6, and the Blazers went home with a runner-up finish that felt enormous and heartbreaking in equal measure. Here is the consolation: losing to those Bulls teams was not shameful. It was practically a rite of passage. Virtually every great team of that era lost to the Bulls at some point. Portland just lost at the very last possible moment, which is the most Portland way to do it.

12. The Jail Blazers: The Most Chaotic Roster in NBA History

Around the year 2000, the Portland Trail Blazers assembled a roster that was, on paper, absolutely loaded with talent. Rasheed Wallace. Scottie Pippen. Damon Stoudamire. Bonzi Wells. Zach Randolph. These were real, legitimate NBA players capable of doing remarkable things with a basketball. The problem, and there is no delicate way to say this, is that collectively they were also capable of doing remarkable things without a basketball, and not all of those things were what the front office had in mind when they signed the checks.

The nickname "Jail Blazers" was not something the team chose for themselves. It was handed to them by a media and fan base that watched a steady stream of off-court incidents, fines, suspensions, and general chaos unfold over several seasons and eventually ran out of more polite ways to describe it. Rasheed Wallace alone set an NBA record for technical fouls in the 2000-01 season that stood for years. He received forty-one technicals. In one season. That is nearly one every other game. Referees reportedly started keeping a Wallace-specific foul counter just to stay organized.

The wildest part of the Jail Blazers story is that the team was actually good. Good enough to reach the 2000 Western Conference Finals against the Lakers, where they built a fifteen-point lead in the fourth quarter of Game 7 before collapsing in one of the most spectacular fourth-quarter meltdowns in NBA playoff history. The Lakers outscored them 15-0 to close the game. Fifteen to nothing. In a Game 7. In the fourth quarter. With a fifteen-point lead. Portland fans have never fully recovered from this, and frankly, who could blame them. That is not a loss. That is a haunting.

13. Brandon Roy's Comeback Game: The Night a Broken Superstar Said "Not Yet"

By April 2011, Brandon Roy's knees were done. Not "a little sore" done. Not "needs some rest" done. Medically, structurally, cartilage-has-left-the-building done. Roy had been one of the most gifted shooting guards in the NBA just a few years earlier, a three-time All-Star who moved and scored with a grace that reminded people of players much more famous than him. But his knees had deteriorated to the point where every game he played was borrowed time, and most basketball people watching understood that his career was effectively winding down whether he wanted it to or not.

Then came Game 4 of the first-round playoff series against the Dallas Mavericks. Portland was down three games to none, which in NBA history essentially means pack your bags because no team had ever come back from 3-0 to win a series. Roy came off the bench, which was a sentence nobody expected to be writing about a former All-Star in his prime. He scored eighteen points in the fourth quarter. Eighteen. In one quarter. On knees that had no business carrying him to the corner, let alone launching him into one of the most extraordinary individual playoff performances anyone had ever seen.

Portland won that game. They did not win the series. The Mavericks closed it out in Game 5, and the Blazers went home. Roy retired a few months later, his body finally winning the argument his will had been refusing to have. But that fourth quarter against Dallas exists as something permanent in Trail Blazers history, a moment so defiant and so human that even Dallas fans who were there have admitted it was something special to witness. Brandon Roy played through circumstances that would have ended most players' nights and nearly pulled off the impossible. Nearly is doing a lot of work in that sentence. But nearly, in this case, was more than enough to remember forever.

14. Dame Time vs. Oklahoma City: The Shot Heard Round Rip City

April 23, 2019. Portland Trail Blazers versus Oklahoma City Thunder. Game 5 of the first round of the playoffs. The series is tied. The game is tied. There are less than two seconds left on the clock. The ball is in Damian Lillard's hands, roughly thirty-seven feet from the basket, which is a distance most NBA players would consider a reasonable place to start thinking about getting closer before attempting a shot.

Damian Lillard did not get closer. Damian Lillard stepped back, caught the inbound pass with the clock expiring, and launched a shot from a distance so far out that several courtside observers reportedly thought he had simply lost his mind. The ball went up. Time ran out. The ball came down. It went through the net with a sound so clean and so final that the entire arena took approximately one full second to process what had just happened before erupting into the loudest noise a building full of human beings is capable of producing.

What happened next became one of the most replayed images in recent NBA history. Lillard turned toward the Oklahoma City bench, specifically toward Russell Westbrook and Paul George, the Thunder's two stars who had spent the series talking about how Portland was not a real threat, and he pointed. Not aggressively. Not rudely. Just directly. The gesture communicated, with remarkable efficiency, approximately three hundred words of very clear messaging in about half a second. Then he walked away. The Blazers won the series. Rip City did not sleep that night. Dame Time was officially, permanently, and completely undeniably real.

15. The Sellout Streak: Portland's Most Quietly Unbelievable Record

Here is a sports record that does not get nearly enough attention nationally but makes Portland fans smile the widest. The Trail Blazers held one of the longest consecutive sellout streaks in major North American professional sports history. Not the longest in the NBA. Not the longest in basketball. In all of major North American professional sports. Football. Baseball. Hockey. Basketball. All of it. Portland was the answer.

The streak ran from 1977, conveniently right after that championship, all the way to 1995. Eight hundred and fourteen consecutive sellouts. That is eighteen years of walking up to the ticket window and being told, with impressive regularity, that there was nothing available.

Eighteen years of Portland packing Memorial Coliseum to see a team that, during various stretches of that streak, was not always what you would generously call a championship contender. It did not matter. Portland showed up anyway.

What makes this record genuinely remarkable, beyond the raw numbers, is what it says about the relationship between a city and its team. Portland does not have an NFL franchise. It does not have an MLB team. For a long stretch of those eighteen years, the Trail Blazers were the only major professional sports team in Oregon, which meant that the entire state poured its energy and its loyalty and its ticket money into one building, one team, one identity. "Rip City" was not just a chant. It was the whole sports culture of an entire state, concentrated into one arena, for eighteen consecutive years without a single empty seat. That is not a record. That is a love story.

Chapter 4: Weird, Wild, and Wonderfully Portland

16. Moda Center: The House That Rip City Built

The Moda Center sits in the Rose Quarter district of Portland, right on the east bank of the Willamette River, and it has been the home of the Trail Blazers since 1995. Before that, Portland played in Memorial Coliseum, which was where the 1977 championship happened and where the sellout streak was born, and which Portland fans still speak about with the kind of fondness usually reserved for a grandparent's kitchen. The Moda Center replaced it not because anyone wanted to leave, but because the 1990s had opinions about arena size and the Trail Blazers needed more seats to sell to the people who were going to fill them anyway.

The arena has gone through a few name changes over the years, which is the corporate sponsorship version of someone moving the furniture around in a house you have lived in for decades. It has been the Rose Garden, then the Moda Center, and Portland fans have handled each transition with the patience of people who understand that the name on the outside does not change what happens on the inside. What happens on the inside, when the Blazers are playing and the building is full, is one of the better basketball atmospheres in the entire league. Loud, passionate, knowledgeable, and occasionally so intense that opposing players have mentioned it in postgame interviews with the facial expressions of people who did not entirely enjoy the experience. Which is exactly what a home court advantage is supposed to feel like.

The Moda Center holds just under twenty thousand fans and has hosted concerts, events, and various other productions over the years, but it is fundamentally a basketball building. It smells like popcorn and feels like anticipation. On a playoff night, with the lights down and the introductions playing and nineteen thousand something people on their feet, it is one of those places that reminds you why live sports exist in the first place. Portland built it, filled it, and has never once taken it for granted.

17. Blaze the Trail Cat: Oregon's Most Enthusiastic Employee

Blaze the Trail Cat is the official mascot of the Portland Trail Blazers, and he is exactly what you would expect from a franchise based in the Pacific Northwest. He is a large anthropomorphic cat wearing a Blazers uniform, with enormous eyes, a permanently enthusiastic expression, and the energy of someone who has consumed an inadvisable amount of espresso and has decided to spend the consequences doing backflips courtside. He is wonderful. He is unhinged in the best possible way. Portland loves him completely.

Blaze was introduced in 2002, which means the Trail Blazers spent their first thirty-two years as a franchise without an official mascot, which raises the reasonable question of what was happening on the sidelines during timeouts all that time. Apparently just cheerleaders and vibes. Blaze arrived and immediately filled a gap nobody had formally identified but everyone recognized the moment he showed up. He does dunks on a trampoline. He interacts with fans in ways that suggest he does not have a volume setting below eleven. He takes his job with a seriousness that is somehow both completely sincere and completely ridiculous, which is the ideal quality in a mascot.

The Trail Cat element of his identity is a fun quirk because the Trail Blazers have never officially been the Trail Cats. The team name is about pioneers and exploration, not felines. But somewhere in the mascot design meeting of 2002, someone said "what if it was a cat though" and the room apparently agreed, and now Portland has a large friendly cat running around the arena making children laugh and occasionally terrifying opposing players who are not expecting to round a corner and encounter him at full enthusiasm. Blaze is a treasure. This point is non-negotiable.

18. The Pinwheel Jersey: The Coolest Uniform Nobody Talks About

In 1969, before the Trail Blazers had even played their first game, someone in the organization sat down to design a logo and a uniform and produced something that the sports fashion world has spent decades quietly appreciating. The Trail Blazers' original logo featured a pinwheel design, a series of lines radiating outward in red, white, and black, that was clean, geometric, bold, and looked absolutely nothing like any other team in professional basketball. It was modern before modern was a design category. It was distinctive before distinctive was considered a goal.

The pinwheel logo and the uniforms built around it have become genuinely iconic in NBA visual history. When the league and various publications rank the greatest uniforms in professional sports, Portland's classic look appears near the top of those lists with a frequency that suggests it was not an accident. The design has been updated and tweaked over the decades, as all uniforms eventually are, but the core identity, the red, the white, the black, the clean geometry, has remained consistent enough that a Trail Blazers jersey from 1977 and a Trail Blazers jersey from 2019 look like they belong to the same family. That kind of visual consistency across fifty years is rarer than it sounds and harder to achieve than it looks.

There is something fitting about a franchise called the Trail Blazers having one of the most forward-thinking visual identities in sports history. They were blazing trails aesthetically as well as literally, which is either a happy coincidence or evidence that whoever founded this team was operating at a level of intentionality that deserves considerably more credit. The pinwheel was not just a logo. It was a statement. It still is.

19. Portland's Superfans: The People Who Bleed Red and Black

Every NBA team has fans. The good franchises have passionate fans. The truly special franchises have superfans, the kind of people who have been coming to games for thirty years, who have a specific seat they consider spiritually theirs, who know the names of the players' dogs, and who would sooner miss a family holiday than a playoff game. Portland has those people in quantities that would make larger market teams quietly jealous if they thought about it long enough.

Part of what creates this level of devotion is geography. Portland is Oregon's city. The whole state claims the

Blazers, which means the fanbase draws from an entire state's worth of passion rather than just a metropolitan area. Kids in Eugene grow up Trail Blazers fans. Families in Bend have Trail Blazers season tickets. The team travels with them, in car radios and living room televisions, across a geography that in other states might support multiple franchises but in Oregon concentrates entirely into one. That concentration produces intensity.

The superfan culture in Portland also has a specific character that feels unique to the Pacific Northwest. It is enthusiastic without being aggressive. It is deeply knowledgeable without being exclusionary. Portland fans will explain the intricacies of the triangle offense to you while offering you locally sourced snacks and recommending a coffee shop near the arena. They care enormously and they are also extremely pleasant about it, which is somehow more intimidating than the alternative. You cannot argue with someone who is both more informed than you and also genuinely happy to see you. Portland has built an entire fanbase on that principle.

20. Fun, Weird, and Completely True Trail Blazers Facts

The Trail Blazers once had a player named Lafayette "Fat" Lever, which is a nickname so magnificently of its era that it could only have existed in the 1980s and deserves to be acknowledged by name in any comprehensive Trail Blazers document. Fat Lever was actually an excellent player, a two-time All-Star who averaged a double-double for multiple seasons, and he carried that nickname with a confidence that suggested he had made peace with it approximately five minutes after it was assigned and never thought about it again.

Portland is the only NBA city in the Pacific Northwest, a fact that sounds straightforward until you consider the geography involved. The nearest NBA team to the Trail Blazers is the Golden State Warriors in San Francisco, roughly six hundred and forty miles away. For context, that is roughly the same distance as London to Edinburgh, or New York to Detroit. Portland does not share its basketball identity with a neighbor. There is no crosstown rivalry, no nearby alternative. In Oregon, you are a Trail Blazers fan. That is simply what you are.

The Blazers also have a truly extraordinary history of drafting players and then watching those players become legends somewhere else. In 1984, Portland had the second overall pick in the NBA Draft and selected center Sam Bowie. With the third pick, the Chicago Bulls selected a shooting guard from North Carolina named Michael Jordan. Sam Bowie had a perfectly respectable NBA career. Michael Jordan became Michael Jordan. Portland fans have been asked about this draft decision approximately once every eleven minutes ever since, and they have handled the question with a grace and a weary patience that honestly deserves its own award.

21. Life After Dame: The Trade That Changed Everything

In the summer of 2023, the Portland Trail Blazers traded Damian Lillard to the Milwaukee Bucks, and the city of Portland handled it the way you would expect a city to handle finding out that the person who had been the face, heart, and general emotional center of their sports identity for eleven years was leaving. Which is to say, not easily, and with a lot of feelings that required time to process.

Lillard had requested a trade, which was his right, and Portland eventually sent him to Milwaukee in a deal that brought back several players and future assets. The basketball logic of the trade was sound enough. The emotional logic was considerably more complicated. Lillard was not just a player in Portland. He was a symbol of what a small market franchise could be when the right person chose to commit to it fully. His departure did not erase that. But it did close a chapter in a way that left the city quiet for a while.

What came after was the thing Portland needed to focus on, and to their credit, the front office did not panic. They did not blow everything up dramatically or make trades that sacrificed the future for a short-term fix. They accepted that rebuilding was the correct path, assembled draft picks and young talent, and started the patient work of building something new. It is not the most exciting process. It does not generate the kind of buzz that Dame Time generated. But franchises that skip the rebuild tend to spend a decade regretting it, and Portland has been around long enough to know that patience, applied correctly, eventually produces something worth the wait.

22. Scoot Henderson: The Kid Who Carries the Future

In the 2023 NBA Draft, Portland selected Scoot Henderson with the third overall pick, and the moment felt like a statement. Not a consolation. Not a "well, this is what rebuilding looks like" move. A genuine, eyes-forward, this-kid-is-special statement about where the Trail Blazers intended to go next. Henderson arrived in Portland as one of the most highly anticipated young players in years, a point guard with athleticism that made scouts run out of adjectives and a competitive drive that NBA people described with the kind of language usually reserved for players who end up on highlight reels for the next fifteen years.

Henderson was nineteen years old when he played his first NBA game. Nineteen. At nineteen, most people are figuring out how a washing machine works and whether ramen constitutes a balanced meal. Scoot Henderson was learning how to guard All-Stars in front of twenty thousand people in a professional basketball arena. The adjustment was real, as it always is for teenage NBA players, but the flashes of what he was capable of were frequent enough and spectacular enough that Portland fans watching closely understood they were seeing the beginning of something rather than the middle or the end.

The comparison that gets made most often, and that Henderson himself handles with the calm of someone who has heard it enough times to have formed a considered opinion, is to Damian Lillard. Not in style exactly, but in role. Portland is asking Henderson to be the next face of the franchise, the next player who makes Rip City feel like the center of the basketball universe, the next reason to believe. That is an enormous thing to ask of a nineteen year old. Henderson's early performances suggested he understood the assignment and was not remotely intimidated by it. Rip City is watching. Rip City is ready to believe again.

23. Why Portland Still Matters: Small Market, Massive Heart

There is a version of the NBA story where only the big markets matter. Where Los Angeles and New York and Boston are the ones that get the stars, fill the arenas, generate the national coverage, and win the championships, and everyone else is just background. Portland has spent fifty-plus years being a very loud, very passionate argument against that version of the story.

The Trail Blazers have never had the luxury of being in a market so large that players come simply because of the city's gravitational pull. Portland has to work for it. It has to build culture, develop loyalty, create an environment where players want to be because of what Portland offers, not just what it pays. And remarkably, consistently, over five decades, it has done exactly that. Players who come to Portland tend to talk about it differently than they talk about other stops in their careers. There is something about the city, the size of it, the way the fans connect with the team, the Pacific Northwest identity that is unlike anywhere else in professional sports, that gets into people and stays.

What Portland represents in the NBA is proof that the sport is bigger than the markets it plays in. That a city of six hundred thousand people can generate championship-level passion, legendary players, iconic moments, and a fanbase that sells out arenas for eighteen straight years. That Rip City is not a consolation prize for not being Los Angeles. It is its own thing, specific and irreplaceable, and the teams that have come through it and the fans that have sustained it deserve to be recognized not as a small market story but as one of the great stories in the history of professional basketball. Full stop.

24. The Culture of the Blazers: Where Basketball Meets Community

The Trail Blazers have always understood something that not every professional sports franchise figures out, which is that a team belongs to a city in a way that goes beyond the games. It is about being present when the cameras are not rolling, being involved in the community in ways that do not require a press release, and treating the relationship between the franchise and the city as something worth tending carefully rather than taking for granted.

Portland as a city has a specific character. It is creative, independent, outdoorsy, socially conscious, and deeply suspicious of anything that feels like it is performing authenticity rather than actually having it. That is a tough room for a professional sports franchise. Portlanders can tell the difference between a team that genuinely cares about their city and a team that is staging a community event for the Instagram post. The Trail Blazers have, over their history, managed to exist in Portland as something that feels genuinely woven into the city rather than simply located there.

Players who have spent time in Portland talk about the city with real affection. Damian Lillard, most famously, chose Portland over and over again when he could have demanded a trade to a bigger market years earlier. Clyde Drexler built his legacy there. Even players who moved on have maintained connections and warm feelings toward the franchise. Some of that is the winning, or at least the competing. Some of it is the coaching and the front office culture at various points. But some of it is simply Portland, which is one of those places that gets into you quietly and then turns out to have been there the whole time.

25. Rip City Forever: What Makes Portland One of the NBA's Most Special Franchises

Here is what you know now that you did not know twenty-five facts ago. The Portland Trail Blazers are a franchise built on unlikely things. An accidental battle cry shouted by a broadcaster who did not know where the words came from. A championship won by a team nobody outside Oregon expected to win anything. A sellout streak maintained through good years and bad ones by fans who showed up because showing up was simply what you did. Buzzer-beaters from distances that should not be attempted. A mascot who is technically a cat despite the team being named after pioneers. A draft pick that became the most famous mistake in NBA history and somehow did not define the franchise because everything else they built was interesting enough to talk about instead.

What the Trail Blazers represent, at their best, is the thing sports are supposed to be. Not just wins and losses, not just rosters and contracts and television ratings, but a genuine connection between a place and a team that runs deeper than logic can fully explain. Portland should not, by the conventional metrics of professional sports success, be one of the NBA's most beloved franchises. It is too small, too far from the center of the media universe, without enough championships to build a dynasty narrative around. And yet here it is. Beloved. Loud. Stubbornly, magnificently present.

Rip City started as an accident. It became an identity. And somewhere right now, in a living room in Eugene or a bar in Bend or an arena on the east bank of the Willamette River, somebody is watching the Trail Blazers play basketball and feeling exactly what Bill Schonely felt in 1971 when he opened his mouth and something true came out. It is not a record. It is not a chant. It is not even really a city. Rip City is what happens when a place decides to love something completely and refuses to stop. That is the whole story. That is Portland. That is the Trail Blazers. And honestly, that is enough.

Bonus Trivia Quiz!

You think you are a true Trail Blazers fan? Try this bonus quiz!

1. What year did the Portland Trail Blazers join the NBA?

A) 1968

B) 1970

C) 1972

D) 1975

2. Who came up with the battle cry "Rip City" and how did it happen?

A) A fan shouted it during the 1977 championship parade

B) Coach Jack Ramsay used it as a team motto during training camp

C) Radio announcer Bill Schonely blurted it out during a game in 1971

D) Bill Walton said it in a postgame interview after winning the title

3. Which team did Portland defeat to win their only NBA Championship in 1977?

A) Los Angeles Lakers
B) Boston Celtics
C) Seattle SuperSonics
D) Philadelphia 76ers

4. What was Bill Walton named after the 1977 championship run?

A) Defensive Player of the Year
B) NBA Finals MVP
C) NBA Most Improved Player
D) All-Star Game MVP

5. Why did Arvydas Sabonis not arrive in Portland until 1995 despite being drafted in 1986?

A) He wanted to finish his college career in Europe
B) He was suspended by the NBA for three seasons
C) The Soviet sports system, injuries, and international basketball politics delayed his arrival
D) He refused to play in Portland until the roster improved

6. How many consecutive sellouts did the Trail Blazers record during their famous streak?

A) 512

B) 650

C) 814

D) 902

7. Clyde Drexler earned his nickname "The Glide" because of what quality?

A) His extremely long arms
B) The fluid, effortless way he moved on the court
C) His ability to glide past defenders off the dribble
D) The way he ran the fast break

8. Which NBA Draft decision is considered the most famous mistake in Trail Blazers history?

A) Passing on Kobe Bryant in 1996 to select Jermaine O'Neal
B) Selecting Sam Bowie second overall in 1984 instead of Michael Jordan
C) Trading away a future Hall of Famer for a second-round pick
D) Passing on Shaquille O'Neal to re-sign a veteran center

9. What record did Rasheed Wallace set during the Jail Blazers era?

A) Most points scored in a single season by a Trail Blazer
B) Most games played without a playoff appearance
C) Most technical fouls in a single NBA season with forty-one
D) Most ejections in a single playoff series

10. How many points did Brandon Roy score in the fourth quarter of his legendary 2011 playoff game against the Dallas Mavericks?

A) Twelve
B) Fifteen
C) Eighteen
D) Twenty-two

11. Approximately how far from the basket was Damian Lillard standing when he hit his series-ending buzzer-beater against Oklahoma City in 2019?

A) Twenty-five feet
B) Twenty-nine feet
C) Thirty-three feet
D) Thirty-seven feet

12. What is the name of the Portland Trail Blazers official mascot?

A) Blaze the Trail Cat

B) Rocky the Blazer

C) Rip the Wildcat

D) Torch the Mountain Lion

13. What was the name of the arena the Trail Blazers played in before the Moda Center?

A) The Rose Palace

B) Memorial Coliseum

C) Pioneer Arena

D) Columbia Center

14. With which overall pick in the 2023 NBA Draft did Portland select Scoot Henderson?

A) First

B) Second

C) Third

D) Fourth

15. Which team did the Trail Blazers famously collapse against in Game 7 of the 2000 Western Conference Finals, blowing a fifteen-point fourth-quarter lead?

A) San Antonio Spurs

B) Utah Jazz

C) Los Angeles Lakers

D) Seattle SuperSonics

Super Fan Secret Challenge

Only a true Trail Blazers fan will know this.

(No Answer Provided)

In the 1984 NBA Draft, Portland selected Sam Bowie with the second overall pick instead of Michael Jordan. But here is what most people do not know. There was actually another future Hall of Fame player selected in that same draft who also went before Jordan. Who was that player, which team selected him, and with which pick did he go?

A) Charles Barkley, Philadelphia 76ers, fifth overall

B) Hakeem Olajuwon, Houston Rockets, first overall

C) John Stockton, Utah Jazz, sixteenth overall

D) Patrick Ewing, New York Knicks, fourth overall

Answer Key

1. B) 1970

2. C) Radio announcer Bill Schonely blurted it out during a game in 1971

3. D) Philadelphia 76ers

4. B) NBA Finals MVP

5. C) The Soviet sports system, injuries, and international basketball politics delayed his arrival

6. C) 814

7. B) The fluid, effortless way he moved on the court

8. B) Selecting Sam Bowie second overall in 1984 instead of Michael Jordan

9. C) Most technical fouls in a single NBA season with forty-one

10. C) Eighteen

11. D) Thirty-seven feet

12. A) Blaze the Trail Cat

13. B) Memorial Coliseum

14. C) Third

15. C) Los Angeles Lakers

NBA PLAYOFF BRACKET

First Round	Semifinals	Conf. Finals	Finals	Conf. Finals	Semifinals	First Round

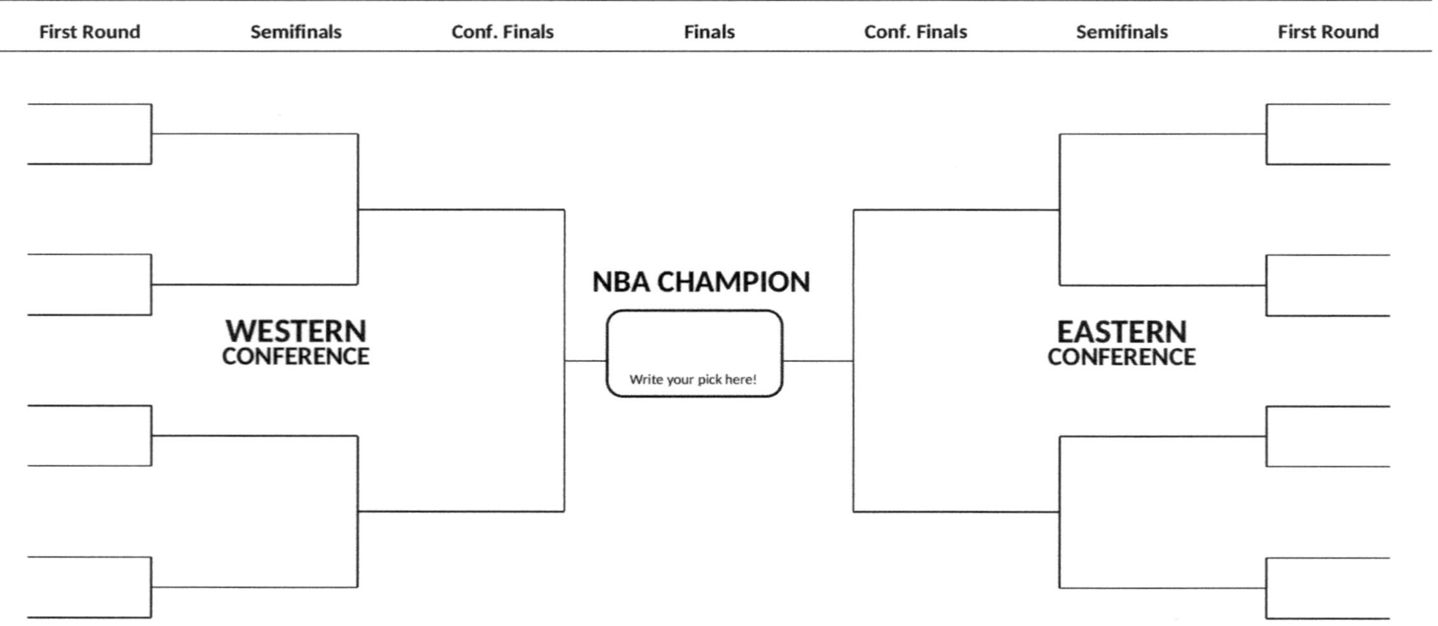

* Fill in your picks and try not to argue with your friends about it!

Part of the Fun Fan Facts: The Unofficial Sports Guide Series

Be the Boss of the Playoffs

You've broken down the matchups. You know which superstar takes over in the fourth quarter. You've seen the bench units that quietly decide series. You've watched the adjustments coaches make when their backs are against the wall.

Now it's time to stop watching and start deciding.

On this page, you are not just a fan. You are the Head Coach drawing up the last play with three seconds left on the clock. You are the GM who built this roster. You are the analyst who saw it all coming.

This is not just filling out a bracket.

This is building your championship run.

Sixteen teams enter the NBA Playoffs. The path is brutal. Best of seven. No shortcuts. No hiding. Every round gets louder, harder, and more personal.

This bracket is your Playoff Control Room.

The Game Plan

1. Survive Round One: Start with the opening round. Which matchup is going seven games? Who has the closer? Who folds under pressure? Make the calls.

2. Feel the Momentum: As you move into the Conference Semifinals and Conference Finals, things change. Role players become heroes. Stars feel the weight. Trust your reads.

3. Own the Finals: Trace your picks all the way to the NBA Finals. When the confetti falls and the trophy is raised, you'll find out who earned it.

House Rules: Circle your boldest upset. That is your official "I knew it" moment.

Choose Your Weapon: Pencil if you want flexibility. Pen if you trust your instincts. Sharpie if you believe in chaos.

Because once the playoffs tip off, there is no rewinding Game 7.

Make your picks. Trust your basketball brain. And let the playoff drama begin.

Fun Facts Wrap-Up

You made it through! You're officially a true superfan! Now it's time to put your knowledge to the test. Share these facts with friends and see who really knows their team best.

Love the series?

Your reviews help other fans discover Fun Fan Facts. If you enjoyed this book, we'd really appreciate you sharing your thoughts and leaving a review.

Want more Fun Fan Facts?

Scan the QR code below to visit our site and explore bonus trivia, challenges, and special extras - including new teams, future series, and collectible fun as they're released.

Collect All the Fun Fan Facts Series!

Check off every book you read. See the full set on Amazon. Search "Fun Fan Facts Jake Liam."

World Cup 2026 Edition

☐ Algeria	☐ Scotland	☐ Morocco
☐ France	☐ Brazil	☐ Switzerland
☐ Paraguay	☐ Ivory Coast	☐ Curaçao
☐ Argentina	☐ Senegal	☐ Netherlands
☐ Germany	☐ Canada	☐ Tunisia
☐ Portugal	☐ Japan	☐ Ecuador
☐ Australia	☐ South Africa	☐ New Zealand
☐ Ghana	☐ Cape Verde	☐ United States
☐ Qatar	☐ Jordan	☐ Egypt
☐ Austria	☐ South Korea	☐ Norway
☐ Haiti	☐ Colombia	☐ Uruguay
☐ Saudi Arabia	☐ Mexico	☐ England
☐ Belgium	☐ Spain	☐ Panama
☐ Iran	☐ Croatia	☐ Uzbekistan

World Cup 2026 Group Edition

☐ Group A	☐ Group F	☐ Group K
☐ Group E	☐ Group J	☐ Group D
☐ Group I	☐ Group C	☐ Group H
☐ Group B	☐ Group G	☐ Group L

English Football Edition

☐ Arsenal F.C.

☐ Aston Villa F.C.

☐ Chelsea F.C.

☐ Everton F.C.

☐ Fulham F.C.

☐ Liverpool F.C.

☐ Manchester City

☐ Manchester United

☐ Newcastle United F.C.

☐ Tottenham Hotspur

☐ West Ham United

☐ Wrexham A.F.C.

NBA Edition

☐ Atlanta Hawks

☐ Boston Celtics

☐ Brooklyn Nets

☐ Charlotte Hornets

☐ Chicago Bulls

☐ Cleveland Cavaliers

☐ Dallas Mavericks

☐ Denver Nuggets

☐ Detroit Pistons

☐ Golden State Warriors

☐ Houston Rockets

☐ Indiana Pacers

☐ LA Clippers

☐ Los Angeles Lakers

☐ Memphis Grizzlies

☐ Miami Heat

☐ Milwaukee Bucks

☐ Minnesota Timberwolves

☐ New Orleans Pelicans

☐ New York Knicks

☐ Oklahoma City Thunder

☐ Orlando Magic

☐ Philadelphia 76ers

☐ Phoenix Suns

☐ Portland Trail Blazers

☐ Sacramento Kings

☐ San Antonio Spurs

☐ Toronto Raptors

☐ Utah Jazz

☐ Washington Wizards

About the Author

Jake is a 13-year-old sports fan who loves football, American football, and basketball. He plays soccer as a goalie and dreams of one day playing for West Ham United and helping teach kids to love the game. His passion for sports runs in the family - his dad was a professional baseball player, and his stepdad sparked his love for West Ham. Through the Fun Fan Facts series, he shares the fun and excitement of sports with fans everywhere.

www.ingramcontent.com/pod-product-compliance
Lightning Source LLC
Chambersburg PA
CBHW050039040726
47599CB00015B/1747